2/5

GIUNTI UNIVERS

THE RENAISSANCE

Text by Elena Capretti

GIUNTI

Translation from italian by Paula Boomsliter for Traduco Snc di Bovone e Bulckaen (Firenze)

PHOTOGRAPHIC CREDITS
Archivio Giunti. Every effort has been made to trace the copyright holders. The editor would be pleased to correct any unintentional omissions for any photographs for which we have been unable to trace the source.

ISBN 88-09-21512-5

Contents

Introduction

When in 1436 Leon Battista Alberti wrote the second edition of his treatise on painting "in the Tuscan language" and dedicated it to Filippo Brunelleschi, he acknowledged both the homeland and the main mover of that which was already being called "*rinascenza*." And today, like in Alberti's time, Brunelleschi, Donatello and Masaccio are considered the originators of the Renaissance. That which these artists designed, sculpted, formed or painted was an expression of a new manner of conceiving Man and Nature and the relationship of the microcosm of the one with the macrocosm of the other, as the philosophers and men of letters of the time theorized. Man, made of soul and body, was placed at the center of the perceptible earthly sphere. There thus arose in him a need to observe, to define and to represent visible and imaginable reality according to empirical-scientific principles, in order to later idealize it or attribute to it symbolic values. All this is revealed by Masaccio in the frescoes in Santa Maria del Carmine in Florence (c. 1427), and is revealed equally, but in a different language, by Jan van Eyck in his polyptych the *Adoration of the Lamb* (1432). The dates are close; one is Florentine, the other Flemish. The *homo novo* of the Renaissance, whether a member of the lay bourgeoisie, interested above all in attaining economic standing, or an aristocrat, interested in giving a more modern face to his estates, continually measured himself against time, life and death. ›

1. Lorenzo Ghiberti, *The Sacrifice of Isaac* (1401). Florence, Bargello.

2. Filippo Brunelleschi, *The Sacrifice of Isaac* (1401). Florence, Bargello.

The two panels are the competition reliefs submitted by Ghiberti and Brunelleschi respectively to the competition held in 1401 for the north portal of the Baptistery. The winner was Ghiberti, whose idealized, serene and harmonious interpretation of the scene won out over the more dramatic and immediate intonation given it by Brunelleschi. Both artists derived inspiration for many of their works from ancient sources.

3. Leonardo da Vinci, *The Proportions of the Human Body* (c. 1490). Venice, Gallerie dell'Accademia.
"The figure described by the body is further divided into two other parts; that is, into the proportionality of the parts themselves, which correspond roughly to the whole, and the movement appropriate to the mental events of the living and moving thing." (Leonardo)

1

2

3

In the Renaissance, art was a laissez-passer to eternity for both the patron and the artist, whose position in society gained in prestige as time went on. Mantegna, Alberti, Raphael, Titian and Dürer were court artists who enjoyed uncommon privileges and received tokens of gratitude of all kinds. The artist had four major concerns: applying perspective in order to represent a three-dimensional subject on a two-dimensional plane; observing nature attentively and with an enquiring eye; studying that history of which Man, having been granted free will, is the protagonist; and finally, rehabilitating the classics. In their different approaches to the visible, the Italian *misura*, the Flemish eye for minute detail, and the Swabian expressionism were the alternatives offered by the European Renaissance, and the combinatory solutions were various. On the other hand, the classical texts, whether literary or figurative, offered an infinity of technical, decorative, iconographic, thematic and philosophical stimuli. The interpretations given to the ancient pagan world were essentially two in number, and are well exemplified in the *cantorie* by Donatello and Luca Della Robbia that once graced Florence's Santa Maria del Fiore and now in the Museo dell'Opera del Duomo: the expressive, "Dionysiac" feeling of the one and the idealized and apparently antithetical "Apollonian" cast of the other. Various acceptations of this duality also set at odds other pairs of figures, such as Botticelli and Leonardo, Raphael and Michelangelo, Dürer and Grünewald.

›

1. Donatello, *Cantoria* (1433-1439). Florence, Museo dell'Opera del Duomo.

2. Luca Della Robbia, *Cantoria* (1432-1435). Florence, Museo dell'Opera del Duomo.

In Florence, while Brunelleschi was completing the cupola of Santa Maria del Fiore, Luca Della Robbia and Donatello were commissioned to produce the *cantorie*, or organ balconies over the doors of the sacristy. The common theme of both works was the last psalm of King David, recounting how the children praised the Lord with their songs, music and dance.

3. Inserted in a perspective grid, the study for the background of the *Adoration of the Magi* (Florence, Uffizi) commissioned by the friars of San Donato in Scopeto in 1481 and left unfinished by the artist when he departed for Milan, has the air of a sketch for a stage setting.

1

LAVDATE EVM IN SONO TVBAE · LAVDATE EVM IN PSALTERIO ET CYTHARA · LAVDATE EVM IN TIMPANO

2

3

Ancient art, with such masterpieces as the *Laocoon*, the *Belvedere Apollo* and the *Farnese Hercules* rediscovered in Rome during the Renaissance suggested the study of the anatomy and the proportions of the human body: man's body became the measure of all things, even architectural design. The city too had to be made to man's measure and was required to embrace the qualities of beauty and functionality. The Renaissance produced many plans for ideal cities; the realizations, however, were few. Perhaps the best known is that of Pienza, commissioned in 1459 by Enea Silvio Piccolomini, then Pope Pius II, of Bernardo Rossellino. The urban plans of the great pre-existing cities – like Urbino, Florence and Rome – were reorganized and enhanced with elegant palaces, the tools of self-celebration of the great families. New religious buildings also arose at the same time, and Italy from Brunelleschi onward saw a growing interest for churches on the central plan (for example, Bramante's *Tempietto* in San Pietro in Montorio in Rome, 1505-1506). The Renaissance developed through three fundamental phases: from the Florentine Humanism of the early *Quattrocento* to the Renaissance proper in the second half of the century, with its center in the refined Laurentian culture, to the Mannerist phase of the early 16th century with its fulcrum set in papal Rome. A clean point of severance with this later so nostalgically remembered modern "Golden Age" came in 1527 with the Sack of Rome. And Luther's voice was already coming in loud and clear. ›

1. Bernardo Rossellino, Pienza (1459-1464). View of the main square. In 1459, Pope Pius II Piccolomini asked Bernardo Rossellino rebuild his native town of Corsignano, near Siena, "from the ground up." The town later took the name of Pienza, after the pope. On the main square stand the church, the Piccolomini Palace and the Borgia Palace symmetrically on the sides, and the Palazzo Pubblico across from the church at the other end of the space.

2. Jacopo della Quercia, *Funeral Monument of Ilaria del Carretto* (1406-1407). Lucca, San Martino. The work, commissioned by Paolo Guinigi at the death of his wife Ilaria in 1405, represents Ilaria lying on the catafalque with a dog (symbol of marital fidelity) at her feet. The work mirrors the refined courtly style in vogue at the court of Burgundy. To this northern inspiration the Psenes Jacopo also added a typically Italian, classical accent, in the putti holding the festoons on the sides of the sarcophagus.

3. Pinturicchio, Piccolomini Library (1592-1508), view showing the 3rd-century sculpture of the *Three Graces*). Siena, Cathedral. Francesco Todeschini Piccolomini, later Pope Pius III, had the library built adjacent to the cathedral of Siena in 1495-1497 to house a splendid collection of illuminated manuscripts. In 1502, Pinturicchio began frescoing the walls with the *Scenes from the Life of Pope Pius II* (Enea Silvio Piccolomini). Among those who collaborated with Pinturicchio was the young Raphael.

1

2

3

Florence

Convention sets the date of the beginning of the Florentine Renaissance at 1401, coincident with the competition for the commission to make the second pair of bronze doors of the Baptistery. The contestants included Brunelleschi and Ghiberti; the theme proposed for the entries, in the form of bronze quatrefoil panels, was *Abraham's Sacrifice of Isaac* (Florence, Bargello). After that date and until the 1470s, while humanistic literary studies abounded, the large craft guilds financed important works, mainly for the major public buildings. Thus, while Santa Maria del Fiore and Giotto's bell-tower were the center of bustling activity under the patronage of the Arte della Lana, the doors of the Baptistery, financed by the Arte dei Mercanti di Calimala, were completed, and the sculptures for the tabernacles on the exterior of the Orsanmichele church, each belonging to a different guild, were commissioned. In the shadow of the rising cupola of Santa Maria del Fiore, built between 1420 and 1437 by Filippo Brunelleschi, the commissions by the powerful Florentine patrician families proliferated: Brunelleschi himself completed the old sacristy of the church of San Lorenzo for Cosimo il Vecchio de' Medici (1422-1428), Gentile da Fabriano painted the altarpiece of the *Adoration of the Magi* for the altar of Palla Strozzi in Santa Trinita, and Masolino and Masaccio frescoed the chapel of Felice Brancacci in Santa Maria del Carmine (1424-1428).

›

1. Gentile da Fabriano, *Adoration of the Magi* (1423); Florence, Uffizi.

2. Domenico Veneziano, *Magnoli Altarpiece* (1445-1447). Florence, Uffizi.

3. The Medici-Riccardi Palace by Michelozzo (1444-1464), corner view of the exterior; Florence.

1

2

3

For a number of years thereafter the international Gothic expressed by Gentile remained a valid alternative to Masaccio's heroic and unadorned humanity. The first to understand Masaccio's message was Beato Angelico, who in the 1440s began to decorate the San Marco convent that had just been restructured by Michelozzo for Cosimo de' Medici. Among the many who worked for Cosimo and his son Piero were Paolo Uccello, Domenico Veneziano, Filippo Lippi and Benozzo Gozzoli. The latter frescoed the aristocratic and magical *Procession of the Magi* in 1459 in the chapel of the Medici-Riccardi Palace, built by Michelozzo in Via Larga. The elegant, ornamental, and in many cases even virtuoso intonation of the art of the latter half of the century is also clearly manifest in the chapel of the Cardinal of Portugal in San Minato al Monte (1461-1466). In the meantime, technique had evolved: bronze casting derived from the ancient Greeks, the highly glazed terracotta reinvented by Luca Della Robbia, the oil painting technique adopted from Flemish art. From 1469 through 1492, the dominant figure on the Florentine and Italian political scene was Lorenzo il Magnifico, the promoter of a progressively more conservative and elitist culture, of neo-Platonic stamp, in an environment that soon became too restrictive for an artist like Leonardo, who in 1482 emigrated to Milan. In the 1480s Lorenzo, a collector of antiquities and precious objects, lent his best artists to the other Italian courts, using them as a sort of manifesto of Florentine prestige. ›

1. Benozzo Gozzoli, *The Procession of the Magi* (1459), detail with the idealized portrait of Lorenzo il Magnifico. Florence, Palazzo Medici Riccardi.

2. Andrea Verrocchio, *Lady with Primroses* (c. 1478). Florence, Bargello.

3. Luca Della Robbia, *The Resurrection* (1444), lunette in glazed terracotta. Florence, Cathedral.

1

2

3

Lorenzo sent Giuliano da Sangallo, his favorite among architects, to Naples; he allowed Andrea Verrocchio, sculptor, painter and goldsmith, and master to Botticelli, Perugino and Leonardo, to go to Venice; to Rome he sent Antonio del Pollaiolo, Botticelli and Ghirlandaio. Lorenzo was not the patron of the Florentine masterpieces of those years. Patrons were instead his cousin Lorenzo di Pierfrancesco, who sponsored Botticelli, the Sassettis and the Tornabuonis, for whom Ghirlandaio frescoed in Santa Trinita and in Santa Maria Novella, and Filippo Strozzi, the Magnifico's rival, who asked Filippo Lippi to decorate his chapel in Santa Maria Novella.

Upon the death of Lorenzo and with the emergence of Girolamo Savonarola and all he stood for, the Medicis were driven out of Florence and the Republic was instituted. Art, intimidated by the severe admonitions of the friar, rediscovered an austerity that had been lost and also acquired a new sense of monumentality and at times even sentimentality: spokesmen of this renewal included Perugino, and later Fra' Bartolomeo, a follower of Savonarola.

During the gonfaloniership of Pier Soderini, Leonardo, Michelangelo and Raphael were all in Florence. Between 1506 and 1508, however, all three of these great artists abandoned the city, to which the Medicis returned only a few years later. To the new generations, Leonardo and Michelangelo left their cartoons for the *Battaglia di Anghiari* and the *Battaglia di Cascina,* which they had been requested to fresco in Palazzo della Signoria.

1. Antonio Rossellino, Antonio and Piero del Pollaiolo, Alessio Baldovinetti, and Luca Della Robbia, the chapel of the Cardinal of Portugal (1461-1466), general view. Florence, San Miniato.

2. Domenico Ghirlandaio, *Portrait of Marsilio Ficino, Cristoforo Landino, Agnolo Poliziano and Demetrio Greco* (1486-1490), detail from the *Scenes from the Lives of the Virgin and Saint John the Baptist.* Florence, Tornabuoni Chapel, Santa Maria Novella.

3. Giuliano da Sangallo, villa of Poggio a Caiano (c. 1485-1513). Poggio a Caiano, near Florence.

1

2

3

Rome

In 1420, pope Martin V reinstated the papacy in Rome and launched the "rebirth" of the city. Gentile da Fabriano and Pisanello, late exponents of International Gothic, came to Rome in those years, as did Masolino and Masaccio from Florence. Following a trip to Florence, where he was welcomed by Cosimo de' Medici, Martin's successor Eugenius IV summoned Beato Angelico to Rome (1443). The friar completed the frescoes of the Chapel of Niccolò in the Vatican under Nicholas V, to whom Leon Battista Alberti dedicated his *De re aedificatoria.* It was from Sixtus IV, made Pope in 1471, that the famous Sistine Chapel built by the Florentine Baccio Pontelli in 1480, took its name. It was decorated in the two years following its completion, with the wall frescoes of the *Stories of Moses and Christ* by Pietro Perugino, Sandro Botticelli, Domenico Ghirlandaio, Cosimo Rosselli, and Luca Signorelli. On 15 August 1483, the Pope inaugurated the chapel and dedicated it to Our Lady of the Assumption. Among the Florentines come to Rome near the end of the century were Antonio del Pollaiolo, the author of the tomb of Sixtus IV in Saint Peter's, and Filippino Lippi, who frescoed the Carafa chapel in Santa Maria sopra Minerva. A pupil of Perugino, Pinturicchio, met with exceptional success in the Rome of the notorious Alessandro VI Borgia. ›

1. Beato Angelico, *The Ordination of Saint Laurence* (1447-1450). Rome, Vatican Palace, Chapel of Niccolò V.

2. Bramante, Tempietto (1505-1506). Rome, San Pietro in Montorio.

3. Pinturicchio, *The Funeral of San Bernardino* (1490). Rome, Santa Maria ad Aracoeli, Bufalini Chapel.

1

2

3

From 1492 through 1494 Pinturicchio frescoed the pope's chambers, drawing his inspiration for the illustrations from astrology and pagan Egypt.

Shortly thereafter, in response to the ferocious accusations launched from Florence against the Borgia pope by Girolamo Savonarola, Luca Signorelli painted a grandiose apocalyptic cycle of frescoes in the Orvieto cathedral in which there appears a raving preacher, the Antichrist.

Cardinal Giuliano della Rovere, who became Pope Julius II in 1503, was a staunch enemy of Borgia. Pope Julius, determined not to live on the same rooms as his rival and predecessor, chose as his papal apartment the rooms on the floor above, and in 1508 had them decorated by Raphael and his able collaborators. That same year, he also summoned Michelangelo to Rome to paint the ceiling of the Sistine Chapel. Donato Bramante had been with the Pope for some time and had begun significant urban restructuring with the aim of making the Vatican the center of the city. In 1506, Julius II had given the okay for construction of the new Saint Peter's Basilica, for which plans by various architects, foremost among whom Bramante himself, Raphael, and Michelangelo, were considered in turn. The axis of art had already shifted from Florence to Rome when the son of Lorenzo il Magnifico, Cardinal Giovanni de' Medici, was elected Pope with the name of Leo X in 1513. The new Pope continued his predecessor's cultural policy, reconfirming Raphael and Michelangelo. But in 1520, when Vatican finances began to dwindle and the Church had begun resorting to the much-criticized sale of indulgences, news came from Germany that Martin Luther had burned the papal bull of excommunication.

1. Melozzo da Forlì, *The Investiture of Platina as Librarian to Pope Sixtus IV* (1477), detached fresco. Rome, Vatican Library.

2. Michelangelo, *Moses* (1515). Rome, San Pietro in Vincoli.

1

2

Urbino and the Renaissance Courts

Thanks to Federico da Montefeltro, duke in 1444, Urbino became one of the most fertile of the Renaissance centers. Federico was one of the most active patrons of the arts in all of Italy. His dream was to build "a city on the form of a palace," as was said at the time, and thirty years later, in 1480, the Ducal Palace was completed by Francesco di Giorgio Martini, from Siena. In the interior, Federico had his private *studiolo* paneled in different woods inlaid in prospective compositions. An aficionado of theatrical performances as well as of philosophical and mathematical studies, Federico organized one of the most complete libraries of the time. Due to his interest in mathematics, furthered by his friendship with Luca Pacioli, he encouraged painting stressing the prospective element, which was perhaps best represented by Piero della Francesca. The Flemish painter Justus of Ghent, the Spaniard Pedro Berruguete, Paolo Uccello, Alberti, Perugino, Melozzo, Bramante and Raphael were all habitués of Montefeltro's marvelous palace. Other courts that became well-known centers of culture and art were Pandolfo Malatesta's Rimini, the Milan of the Sforzas and Ludovico il Moro, the Mantova of the Gonzagas (Mantegna's patrons) and finally Ferrara under the Este family, where in about 1469 Borso d'Este commissioned one of the most important cycles of frescoes in northern Italy: *The Months* in Palazzo Schifanoia, the work of Cosmè Tura, Francesco del Cossa and Ercole de Roberti.

1. Urbino, Ducal Palace (1466-1480. View of the loggia on the Terrazza del Gallo and of the southwest "tower."

2. Andrea Mantegna, *The Triumph of Caesar* (c. 1501), detail. Hampton Court (London), Royal Collections.

3. Francesco del Cossa, the month of *March*, detail of *The Months* in the upper register of the east wall (c. 1470). Ferrara, Palazzo Schifanoia, Salone dei Mesi.

1

2

3

Venice and the Veneto Region

Venice, long constrained by its Byzantine traditions, broke with its policy of estrangement toward the events of the Italian peninsula and began expansion on dry land only after the conquest of Constantinople by the Turks in 1453. Meanwhile, in nearby Padua, classical studies flourished and the Florentine Renaissance made itself felt when Donatello, Filippo Lippi and Paolo Uccello sojourned in the city. This was the milieu in which Andrea Mantegna was trained halfway through the century. Giovanni Bellini and Vittore Carpaccio, in Venice, were strongly influenced by the arrival, in 1475-1476, of Antonello da Messina, who acted as a sort of *trait d'union* between the severe lexicon of Piero della Francesca and the Flemish "eye." The canvases painted by Carpaccio between 1490 and 1510, narrative series for the headquarters of the guilds and confraternities, mirror the affluent mercantile society of the Venice of the times: examples include the cycle of *Scenes from the Life of Saint Ursula*, now in the Gallerie dell'Accademia, and the canvases conserved in San Giorgio degli Schiavoni. It was during the same period that Mauro Codussi built Santa Maria Formosa, San Giovanni Crisostomo, and the Vendramin and Correr palaces, all with an eye to the classicism promoted by Alberti. Meanwhile, in 1507, in the Fondaco dei Tedeschi (the German Exchange), Giorgione and the emerging Titian gave a decisive impulse to painting by adopting the technique of building up images through color without recourse to an underlying sketch. Titian's rapid rise forced the dissident, introverted Lorenzo Lotto out of the picture.

1. Lorenzo Lotto, *Portrait of Bernardo de' Rossi* (1519). Naples, Capodimonte.

2. Giovanni Bellini, *San Giobbe Altarpiece* (c. 1487). Venice, Gallerie dell'Accademia.

3. Titian, *The Assumption* (1516-1518). Venice, Santa Maria Gloriosa dei Frari.

4. Vittore Carpaccio, *The Triumph of Saint George* (1502-1507). Venice, School of San Giorgio degli Schiavoni.

1

2

3

4

Low Countries

After Philip the Good had decided to move his court to Bruges, the Low Countries enjoyed a period of florid economic and cultural development, thanks also to the powerful trade guilds and the presence of influential Italian bankers. The fathers of Flemish Renaissance painting were the Master of Flemalle (perhaps identifiable as Robert Campin) and Jan van Eyck. In about 1420 these two artists set as their primary objective that of achieving in their painting a detailed representation of the visible world, permeated with rich medieval symbolism. The lesson taught by the Master of Flemalle was heard far and wide, especially in the south of Germany and France, in Switzerland, and in Austria. His direct heir was Rogier van der Weyden of Tournai, who painted intensely dramatic works such as the *Deposition* in the Prado (Madrid), datable to about 1435. Van Eyck's school was more local than not, centered on Bruges; of his pupils, the closest to the master was Petrus Christus. Other Flemish painters of note were Hans Memling, Justus of Ghent and Hugo van der Goes, all authors of many works that reached Italy. In the early years of the new century the most important centers of the Flemish school had become Antwerp and Brussels. An engraver, Lucas van der Leyden, worked in provincial Holland. And meanwhile van der Goes was beating time for Hieronymus Bosch, Joachim Patinir and Pieter Brueghel the Elder.

1. Hugo van der Goes, *The Portinari Triptych* (1475-1477), detail. Florence, Uffizi.

2. Rogier van der Weyden, *The Deposition of Christ* (c. 1435). Madrid, Prado.

3. Master of Flémalle, *Annunciation with Saint Joseph and Donors* (c. 1420). New York, Metropolitan Museum.

1

2

3

The Rest of Europe

By about 1430, Flemish art had become a fundamental point of reference for all of northern Europe: ideas and works circulated thanks to the close trade relations with the major cities of other countries, supported by the wealthy Flemish middle class. In Spain, Luis Dalmau was among the first in Europe to demonstrate his debt to van Eyck in his *Virgin of the Councillors*, dated 1449 (Barcelona, Museum of Catalan Art). He was followed by Bartolomé Bermejo, trained in Bruges and leaning toward that strong sentimentalism which was to become a dominant note in later Spanish art. Jaime Huguet, a polished artist active above all in Catalonia, also enjoyed great success. In France, the realistically detailed vision of the Flemish painters often blended quite felicitously with Italian taste for the monumental and classicism: exemplary of such a union is the triptych of the *Annunciation* (Aix-en-Provence, Église de la Madeleine) commissioned in 1442 of that painter known as the Master of Aix. Enguerrand Charonton (perhaps the Master of the Pietà of Avignon, from the work of the same name now in the Louvre) worked in the south. The founder of French Humanism was Jean Fouquet, a miniaturist and painter from Tours; between 1444 and 1447 he was perhaps in Italy, as were many other French painters, at the Neapolitan court of Renato d'Anjou. ›

1. Jaime Huguet, *Polyptych of Saints Adone and Senén* (1459), detail. Terrasa, Museo de Santa Maria.

2. Albrecht Dürer, *The Knight, Death and the Devil* (1513-1514), copper-plate engraving.

3. Hans Holbein the Younger, *Erasmus of Rotterdam*. Paris, Louvre.

4. Jean Fouquet, *The Virgin of Melun*. Antwerp, Musées Royaux des Beaux Arts.

1

2

3

4

In the 16th century, the campaigns conducted by Charles VIII and his successors opened France to the arrival of Italian artists, foremost among whom Leonardo. Civilian architecture, especially that of the chateaux of the Loire, was the first sector to feel the influence of these "imported" artists, as is clearly evinced by Chambord, begun in 1519.

In Germany, overtures to Flemish art were made first in the border areas: in Geneva with Konrad Witz, author of the famous altarpiece of the *Miraculous Draught of Fishes,* dated 1444 (Geneva, Musée d'Art et d'Histoire); in Colmar, with Martin Schongauer, famous primarily as an engraver; in Tyrol with Michael Pacher, an original sculptor and painter whose style, like that of Fouquet in France, was an extraordinary blend of northern and Italian art. With the coming of the new century Germany enjoyed a fertile season of the arts dominated by Albrecht Dürer and Hans Holbein and by Lucas Cranach and Matthias Grünewald, strong personalities torn between the allure of classicism and their attachment to the expressionist tradition. The deep spiritual lacerations of these years are reflected, for example, in Grünewald's *Isenheim Altarpiece,* dated c. 1510 (Colmar, Musée d'Unterlinden). The major artistic centers of the time were between Strasbourg and Freiburg, Ratisbon and Vienna, and in Augusta, the home of the Fugger family of bankers.

In England, in the Quattrocento, civilian architecture was the first to timidly reveal forms and types alternative to those of the Middle Ages, as in the case of the Colleges of Oxford and Cambridge. But the Renaissance truly reached London only with the arrival of the Florentine Pietro Torrigiani, who in 1512-1518 fashioned the tomb of Henry VII and his consort in Westminster Abbey.

1. Konrad Witz, *The Miraculous Draught of Fishes* (1444). Geneva, Musée d'Art et d'Histoire.

2. Matthias Grünewald, *The Isenheim Altarpiece* (1515). Colmar, Musée d'Unterlinden.

1

2

Filippo Brunelleschi

The Florentine architect and sculptor Brunelleschi was as sharp and quick-witted as he was pale and slight, and was the initiator of a new manner of conceiving of art and the figure of the artist. From his early training onward, Filippo di ser Brunelleschi was drawn to study of antiquity; he is thought to have traveled to Rome with Donatello. All of his work is based on his studies of late ancient and Tuscan Romanesque art. In 1401 he faced off against Ghiberti in the competition for the second pair of doors for Florence's Baptistery, and for another competition sculpted the wooden *Crucifix* in the Gondi chapel in Santa Maria Novella in parallel with that by Donatello in Santa Croce. He spent a goodly part of his life as an architect (1417-1436), working on the cupola of Florence's Santa Maria del Fiore and at the same time on many other buildings in the city, first of all the Spedale degli Innocenti, the foundling asylum commissioned by the Arte della Seta and begun in 1419. Repudiating the figure of the medieval master builder and donning the garb of the modern architect-engineer and entrepreneur, Brunelleschi addressed two fundamental themes in religious architecture: the cross plan basilica layout, which he used for the churches of San Lorenzo (c. 1420) and Santo Spirito (c. 1436), and the central plan, of classical origin, used for the old sacristy of San Lorenzo (1419-1428) and for the Pazzi chapel in Santa Croce (c. 1430).

Filippo di ser Brunelleschi Lapi, called Brunelleschi (Florence, 1377-1446)

1. Santo Spirito (plan dated c. 1436), interior. Florence.

2. Spedale degli Innocenti (begun in 1419). Florence.

3. Old Sacristy of San Lorenzo (1422-1428). Florence.

4. San Lorenzo (plan dated c. 1420), view of the interior. Florence.

1

2

3

4

Masaccio

This son of the notary Giovanni Cassai of San Giovanni Valdarno is mentioned in Florentine documents dated 1418 as a *"pittore."* His given name was Tommaso, but he was called by the affectionate nickname of Masaccio due to his sloppiness in dress and manner that was, however, compensated by the generosity of his character. While he was still very young, this *enfant prodige* applied to painting that prospective with which Brunelleschi and Donatello had previously experimented in architecture and in sculpture. Despite this, he often worked alongside an older fellow-countryman of his, a late exponent of the Gothic tradition: Masolino da Panicale. Masaccio's masterpiece is in fact the cycle of frescoes in the Brancacci Chapel in Santa Maria del Carmine (1424-1427), which had been begun by Masolino. During those crucial years Masaccio also worked on the polyptych for the Carmelite church in Pisa (1426), now dismembered (the central panel is in the National Gallery of London). This work was followed by the fresco of the *Trinity* in Santa Maria Novella, in the architectural background which it has been suggested that Brunelleschi had a hand – at least as a consultant. In the spring of 1428, Masaccio joined his friend Masolino in Rome, where he is believed to have begun the frescoes of the San Clemente basilica, and he died shortly thereafter, no later than June of the same year.

Tommaso di ser Giovanni di Monte Cassai, called Masaccio (San Giovanni Valdarno, 1401 - Rome, 1428)

1. *Madonna with Child,* part of the polyptych for the Carmine church of Pisa (1426). London, National Gallery.

2. *The Crucifixion,* part of the polyptych for the Carmine church of Pisa (1426). Naples, Capodimonte.

3. *The Adoration of the Magi,* part of the polyptych for the Carmine church of Pisa (1426). Berlin, Staatliche Museen.

1

2

3

Donatello

Donatello collaborated with Ghiberti on the second door of the Florentine Baptistery, and was shortly thereafter employed in making sculptures for the bell-tower and the cathedral, all now in the Museo dell'Opera del Duomo. His early period also includes some works for the exterior of Orsanmichele, among which *Saint George* (Florence, Bargello). In 1423-1427 he sculpted the *Feast of Herod* for the baptismal font of the Baptistery of Siena. In 1432-1433 he made a study trip to Rome, where he was attracted above all by late ancient art. Following that experience he produced the bronze *David* (Florence, Bargello), the *Annunciation* in Santa Croce, the bronze doors for the Old Sacristy of San Lorenzo with the dramatically expensive depiction of apostles and martyrs – which was not to Brunelleschi's liking and contributed to the estrangement of the two old friends. In 1433, Donatello was summoned to Padua to make the monument to Erasmo da Narni, called Gattamelata (1446-1450). He remained at length in the Venetian city, where in 1446 he began work on the altar of the basilica of the Sant'Antonio. In the Fifties, he sculpted *Judith and Holophernes* (Florence, Palazzo Vecchio), and a penetrating wooden *Magdalen* for the Baptistery (Florence, Opera del Duomo). Donatello was honored with burial in the crypt of San Lorenzo, an acolyte in the Pantheon of the Medici family.

Donato di Niccolò di Betto Bardi, called Donatello (Florence, 1386 - 1466)

1. *Saint George* (1417), detail. Florence, Bargello.

2. *San Ludovico d'Angiò, Madonna with Child,* and *San Prosdocimo* from the high altar of the Padua's Basilica of Sant'Antonio (1444-1449).

3. *The Feast of Herod* (1423-1425). Siena, detail of the baptismal font of the Baptistery.

4. *Judith and Holophernes* (1458-1460). Florence, Palazzo Vecchio.

1

2

3

4

Beato Angelico

Guido di Pietro – later given the title Beato Angelico by nineteenth-century literature – is mentioned as a *"pittore"* in 1417, a short while before he entered the monastery of San Domenico in Fiesole with the name of Fra' Giovanni. Influenced by Masaccio and at the same time constrained by his religious commitment, Angelico was the greatest painter in the Florence of the 1430s: both the *Linaioli Altarpiece* (1433), enclosed in a marble shrine by Ghiberti, and the *San Marco Altarpiece* (1438) date to this period. The two works are now in the Museo di San Marco, as are the majority of the artist's creations. The museum is in the former Dominican monastery restructured by Michelozzo for Cosimo del Vecchio, the decoration of which was directed by Angelico and in part executed by the master himself between 1438 and 1442. Angelico had been in San Marco for some years when, after 1445, he made several trips to Rome; by 1450 he had frescoed the Chapel of Niccolò V in the Vatican with *Scenes from the Lives of Saints Stephen and Laurence.* In the meantime he had abandoned, unfinished, the decoration of the San Brizio chapel in the Orvieto cathedral. In Florence, he was prior of San Marco from 1450 through 1452. He died in Rome on 18 February 1455. Historical sources celebrate the humble and devout personality of Beato Angelico, the master who was moved to tears whenever he painted a crucifix.

Guido di Pietro, later Fra' Giovanni da Fiesole, called Beato Angelico (Vicchio di Mugello, Florence, c. 1395 - Rome, 1455)

1. *The Transfiguration* (1439-1445). Florence, Monastery of San Marco.

2. *The Annunciation* (c. 1424). Cortona, Museo Diocesana.

3. *The Deposition* (c. 1440), detail. Florence, Museo di San Marco.

4. *Saint Laurence Giving Alms to the Poor* (1447-1450). Rome, Vatican Palace, Chapel of Niccolò V.

1

2

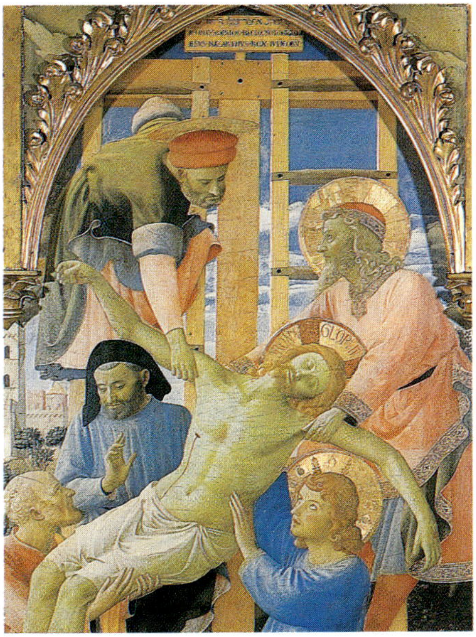

3

4

Jan van Eyck

The Flemish artist Jan van Eyck was the unchallenged protagonist of one of the most important chapters in European Renaissance art, so much so as to have been mentioned by Giovanni Santi, Raphael's father, in his *Cronaca Rimata* on the artists of the time. Having left the court of John of Bavaria, count of Holland, in the Hague, where he is known to have been active from 1422 through 1424, van Eyck went to work for Philip II duke of Burgundy, for whom he also performed diplomatic missions. In Tournai, in 1427, he came into contact with the other protagonists of the Flemish art of that era: Robert Campin and Rogier van der Weyden. Upon his return from Portugal, where he had been sent secretly by the duke in 1428, he made Bruges his permanent home. Following a probable debut as miniaturist, in 1432 he completed the great polyptych for the Church of Saint Bavon in Ghent, which had been left unfinished by his brother Hubert on his death in 1426. The work aroused the admiration of Philip II of Flanders: he would have had it for himself, but since he could not remove it from the city, he had a copy made. Art truer than life, that of van Eyck, as is clearly visible in, for example, the double portrait *Giovanni Arnolfini and his Wife*, painted in 1434 (London, National Gallery) and the *Madonna of the Chancellor Rolin* (Paris, Louvre). It was once thought that van Eyck was the inventor of oil painting. The truth of the matter is that the artist only perfected an already known technique in such a manner as to improve the lighting effects and to so increase the naturalism of the image.

Jan van Eyck (Maastricht?, c. 1390 - Bruges, 1441)

1. *Giovanni Arnolfini and his Wife* (1434). London, National Gallery.

2. *Ghent Altarpiece* (1432). Ghent, Saint Bavon (Gent, Sint Baafs).

3. *Ghent Altarpiece*, detail of Adam.

4. *Ghent Altarpiece*, detail of the *Adoration of the Mystical Lamb.*

1

2

3

4

Piero della Francesca

The young Piero had the opportunity make the first-hand acquaintance of the Florentine art of the late 1430s, since documentary evidence dates his arrival in the city at 1439. He studied primarily Masaccio, Beato Angelico and Domenico Veneziano. Piero never returned to the Tuscan city, but did make periodic journeys to the greatest courts of central Italy. In 1451 he was summoned to Rimini, where he frescoed *Sigismondo Malatesta Before St. Sigismund* in the Tempio Malatestiano. He also went to Ferrara, where he painted frescoes (now lost) in the Este castle and in the Church of Sant'Agostino. Until about 1462 he worked on the cycle of *The Legend of the True Cross* in San Francesco in Arezzo, having accepted, in 1452, to continue the opus initiated by Bicci di Lorenzo and left unfinished at his death. Again in the Arezzo area, he painted the *Madonna del Parto* in the chapel of the Monterchi cemetery and the *Resurrection* in Sansepolcro (Museo Civico).In the 1470s, Piero was very active in Urbino at the court of the Montefeltro family, for whom he had previously painted the diptych now in the Uffizi with the *Portrait of Federico da Montefeltro* and the *Portrait of Battista Sforza*: the complex iconography of the *Madonna and Child with Federico da Montefeltro* (Brera, Milan, dated 1472-1474) the artist's ultimate work, was the fruit of the mathematical Humanism promoted at court by Federico. When he went blind, Piero dedicated his energies to the formulation of treatises on geometry and perspective.

Piero della Francesca (Borgo San Sepolcro, Arezzo, 1415/1420 - 1492)

1. *The Baptism of Christ* (1448-1450). London, National Gallery.

2. *The Meeting of Solomon and the Queen of Sheba* (1452-1466), detail of the *Legend of the True Cross*. Arezzo, San Francesco.

3. *Portrait of Battista Sforza* (c. 1465). Florence, Uffizi.

4. *Portrait of Federico da Montefeltro* (c. 1465). Florence, Uffizi.

1

2

3

4

Sandro Botticelli

A man of restless nature, with a craving for knowledge and experience, Alessandro Filipepi, Florentine, was placed by his father Mariano as apprentice to a certain Botticello, goldsmith, from whom the young artist took the name by which he is universally known. Painting soon revealed itself as Sandro's true vocation, and he became the pupil first of Filippo Lippi and then of Andrea del Verrocchio. In 1470 he opened his own *bottega* and began to frequent the Medici court circles, where he worked at length and became a rather important figure. The literary and philosophical climate of which Lorenzo il Magnifico was the promoter is reflected in the *Primavera*, in *Pallas and the Centaur* and in *The Birth of Venus*, all in the Uffizi, all dated between the late 1470s and the early 1480s, and probably all commissioned by Lorenzo di Pierfrancesco de' Medici. Botticelli was among the artists sent to Rome in 1481 by il Magnifico at Sixtus IV's summons, to fresco the Sistine Chapel. From the end of the century and above all following the death of Lorenzo il Magnifico and the emergence of Girolamo Savonarola, Botticelli was invested by a profound personal religious crisis. This state is clearly expressed in the *Pietà* in the Museo Poldi-Pezzoli in Milan and that of the Alte Pinakothek in Munich, and in the *Mystic Nativity* dated 1501 (London, National Gallery). Once a boisterous, outgoing personality, however unkempt in his ways, Botticelli ended his days as a lonely old man so sick that he could walk only with the aid of two canes.

Sandro Filipepi called Botticelli (Florence 1445 - 1510)

1. The *Madonna of the Pomegranate* (1487). Florence, Uffizi.

2. *The Birth of Venus*. Florence, Uffizi.

3. *Mystic Nativity* (1501). London, National Gallery.

4. *Pietà* (c. 1490). Milan, Museo Poldi-Pezzoli.

1

2

3

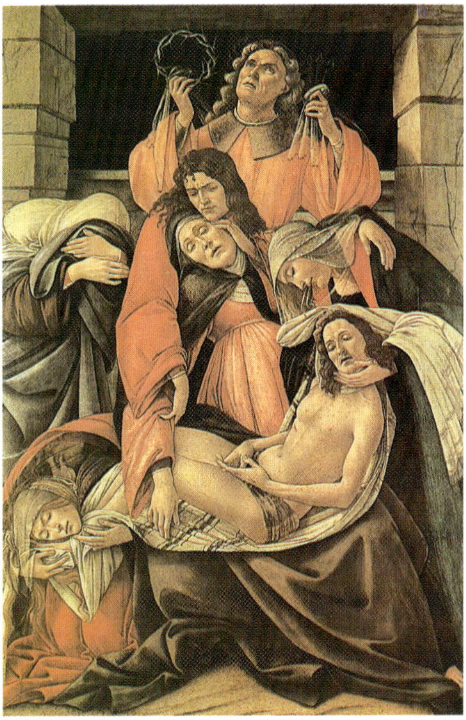

4

Andrea Mantegna

When he came to Padua from his hometown near Vicenza, this son of the woodworker Biagio was adopted by Master Francesco Squarcione, a mediocre painter but a passionate collector. It was in his studio that Mantegna discovered ancient art and developed an interest in the Tuscan artists who had come to the Veneto region. His friendship with Squarcione dissolved, however, when Andrea became the brother-in-law of the Venetian Giovanni Bellini, who Squarcione detested.In 1448, Mantegna and Niccolò Pizzolo began work on the frescoes of the Ovetari chapel in the Eremitani Church in Padua, an opus that was to last through 1459. The theatrical illusionism of these frescoes return, together with a vivid interest in Donatello, in the *San Zeno Altarpiece* painted in 1456-1460 (Verona, San Zeno). In 1460, Mantegna moved to Mantua where he was appointed court artist the Gonzagas and *cavaliere*. Between 1465 and 1474 he decorated the *Wedding Chamber* in the ducal palace; by 1501 he had completed nine canvases depicting the *Triumph of Caesar* (Hampton Court, London, Royal Collections) that won high praise from Ercole I d'Este, duke of Ferrara, and from Francesco Gonzaga. Held in the highest esteem by his patrons until his death, Mantegna left Padua for a longish period for the first time only between 1488 and 1490, when he was summoned to Rome by Pope Innocent IV. In 1497, he painted two canvases (Paris, Louvre) for the *studiolo* of Isabella d'Este in the castle of San Giorgio in Mantua.

Andrea Mantegna (Isola di Carturo, Padua, 1421 - Mantua, 1506)

1. *San Zeno Altarpiece* (1456-1460), detail. Verona, San Zeno.

2. *The Agony in the Garden* (1455). London, National Gallery.

3. *Wisdom Overcoming the Vices* (1502). Paris, Louvre.

1

2

3

Giovanni Bellini

Giovanni Bellini began his apprenticeship in his native Venice under his father Jacopo and together with his brother Gentile. Quite different in temperament from his brother-in-law Andrea Mantegna, early on he matched himself against the latter in works on the same subject, such as the *Agony in the Garden* (London, National Gallery). Bellini shows us an elegiac vision of a sensuous nature populated by a pensive and enigmatic mankind. From the time of the *Pesaro Altarpiece* (1471-1474; Pesaro, Museo Civico, and Rome, Pinacoteca Vaticana) onward, Bellini revealed a sharp interest in Piero della Francesca and in Flemish painting. The mysterious *Sacred Allegory* in the Uffizi was the reflection of a profitable exchange with Antonello da Messina. In 1483, Bellini became the official painter of the Venetian Republic and, thanks to a *bottega* of collaborators as able as they were prolific, managed to fill even the pressing orders for portraits and paintings for the private chambers of the wealthy Venetian middle class. In the first years of the new century, in open competition with Giorgione, Bellini alternated monumental compositions like the *San Zaccaria Altarpiece* (Venice, San Zaccaria) with many variations on the theme of the *Madonna with Child* and with narrative subjects such as the *Feast of the Gods* (Washington, National Gallery) painted in 1514 for the *studiolo* of Alfonso I d'Este in Ferrara.

Giovanni Bellini (Venice, c. 1432 - 1516)

1. *The Madonna of the Meadow* (c. 1505). London, National Gallery.

2. *Portrait of Doge Leonardo Loredan* (1501). London, National Gallery.

3. *Pesaro Family Altarpiece* (c. 1470-1473). Pesaro, Museo Civico.

1

2

3

Albrecht Dürer

Son of a goldsmith, Dürer learned to use the burin early in life, and in later years worked as both a painter and an engraver. Between 1490 and 1494 he made many trips that contributed to his training: to various German cities, to Colmar, where he met the great engraver Martin Schongauer, to Basil, where he co-illustrated several books, and finally to northern Italy and to Venice. Upon his return he opened a workshop in Nuremberg and inaugurated a flourishing production of wood-cuts (the *Apocalypse* and the *Great Passion* series) and paintings, including several self-portraits. Between 1505 and 1507, Dürer was back in Venice painting the great altarpiece *The Feast of the Rose Garlands* (Prague, Národní Galerie) for the funeral chapel of the Germans in the church of San Bartolomeo. Back in Germany, from 1512 onward he dedicated most of his time to engraving. The copperplate engravings of 1513-1514 are justly famous: *The Knight, Death and the Devil*, *St. Jerome in His Study*, and *Melencolia I*.

In 1515, Dürer entered the service of emperor Maximilian I; in 1520, he went to Holland to the court of the new emperor Charles V. This was a profitable trip that was described by Dürer in his diary, which also contains many detailed and realistic drawings, as having offered him the occasion to study Flemish art first-hand. When he returned to Germany, in failing health, he dedicated his energy mostly to theoretical and scientific writings. Dürer died on 6 April 1528 of malaria; to the city he deeded the *Four Apostles*, a work of 1526 (Munich, Alte Pinakothek).

Albrecht Dürer (Nuremberg, 1471-1528)

1. *Self-Portrait* (1500). Munich, Alte Pinakothek.

2. *The Feast of the Rose Garlands* (1506). Prague, Národní Galerie.

3. *Four Apostles* (1526). Munich, Alte Pinakothek.

4. *Adam and Eve* (1504), engraving.

1

2

3

4

Leonardo da Vinci

Leonardo was the natural son of the notary ser Piero da Vinci; in 1469 he followed his father to Florence and entered the *bottega* of Andrea del Verrocchio. He began work as an independent painter in 1472; his early works include the *Annunciation* (Florence, Uffizi), the *Portrait of Ginevra de' Benci* (Washington, National Gallery), and the *Madonna Benois* (Saint Petersburg, Hermitage). In 1481 the monks of San Donato a Scopeto commissioned an *Adoration of the Magi* (Florence, Uffizi), which Leonardo left unfinished when he moved to Milan. The *Virgin of the Rocks* in the Louvre and the fresco of the *Last Supper* were painted in Santa Maria delle Grazie (Milan) between 1495 and 1498. The Milanese milieu was from the first congenial to Leonardo, since it permitted him to pursue his manifold interests: sculpture, hydraulic and military engineering, architecture and town planning, scene design and scientific research. But he fled Milan in 1499, and in 1501 he was again in Florence, where shortly thereafter he began work on the *Mona Lisa* (Paris, Louvre). The second Milanese period dates to between 1506 and 1513; one of the works of this period is the *Virgin and Child with Saint Anne* (Paris, Louvre). In 1513 he spent a brief period in Rome with Pope Leo X de' Medici. In 1517 he was called to France by Francis I, who appointed him "*premier peintre, architecte et méchanicien du roi*" and assigned to him the Cloux castle as his residence.

Leonardo di ser Pietro da Vinci (Vinci, Florence, 1452 - Chateau de Cloux, Amboise, 1519)

1. *Mona Lisa* (1505-1514). Paris, Louvre.

2. *The Virgin with Saint Anne, the Child and the Infant Saint John*, cartoon for *The Virgin and Child with Saint Anne* (c. 1497). London, National Gallery.

3. *The Benois Madonna* (1483-1490). Saint Petersburg, Hermitage.

4. *The Virgin of the Rocks* (1483). Paris, Louvre.

1

2

3

4

Raphael

Raphael began his training in his native Urbino under the aegis of his father Giovanni Santi, painter at the Montefeltro court. After having become an independent *maestro*, Raphael worked in Città di Castello from 1500 through 1504.

That same year went to Florence before the gonfaloniere Pier Soderini with a letter of presentation signed by Giovanna Feltria della Rovere, duchess of Urbino. Although he stayed in the Tuscan city until 1508, he never broke off his working relationships with Urbino and Perugia.

In 1508, Raphael moved to Rome to decorate the apartments of Pope Julius II; his talents were employed by Julius' successor Leo X as well, until the end of his life. Overwhelmed with commissions, Raphael soon employed the services of an excellent team of artists. Raphael was appointed architect of the new Saint Peter's basilica following Bramante's death in 1514, and also superintendent of Rome's antiquities. Among the most prestigious of his patrons in papal Rome were the Sienese banker Agostino Chigi, one of his many works for whom were the frescoes of the loggia of the Farnesina villa.

When Raphael died on 6 April 1516, the entire papal court went into mourning. Some have advanced the theory that his death was due to the immoderate eroticism in which this most important court artists of the period was said to indulge. Raphael left a substantial estate, valued at 16,000 ducats.

Raffaello di Giovanni Santi, called Raffaello Sanzio or Raphael (Urbino, 1483 - Rome, 1520)

1. *The Transfiguration of Christ* (1518-1520). Rome, Pinacoteca Vaticana.

2. *The Madonna del Prato* (1506). Vienna, Kunsthistorisches Museum.

3. *Portrait of Pope Julius II* (1511-1512). London, National Gallery.

4. *The Entombment of Christ* from the Baglioni Altarpiece (*Borghese Deposition*). Rome, Galleria Borghese.

1

2

3

4

Giorgione

We possess little information about the life of Giorgio di Castelfranco, called Giorgione due to the greatness of both his person and his heart. He was one of the artists most highly esteemed by the sixteenth-century literary sources, on a par with Mantegna, Leonardo, Raphael and Michelangelo. He may have been a pupil of Giovanni Bellini and it is certain that he studied the works of Antonello da Messina, Dürer and Leonardo. Giorgione was of humble origins, but in Venice as in Padua he was admitted to the exclusive humanistic circles where the elite dabbled in poetry, literature, philosophy and music.

The altarpiece of the *Madonna and Child with Saints Liberale and Francesco* is an early work in the cathedral of the artist's native city of Castelfranco Veneto. There followed the *Three Philosophers* (Vienna, Kunsthistorisches Museum) and *The Tempest* (Venice, Gallerie dell'Accademia), works of difficult interpretation in which Giorgione expressed an intimate, poetic relationship between man and nature. Among the portraits attributed to him - fascinating and mysterious, with strong psychological and sentimental overtones - are the so-called *Portrait of Laura*, dated 1506 (Vienna, Kunsthistorisches Museum), the *Portrait of a Man* (San Diego, Museum of Art), and the *Portrait of an Old Woman* (Venice, Gallerie dell'Accademia), which is perhaps a portrayal of the artist's mother. In 1507-1508 Giorgione was busy frescoing the exterior of the Fondaco dei Tedeschi with the assistance of the young Titian. Giorgione died of the plague in 1510.

Giorgio Torsi or Giorgio di Castelfranco called Giorgione (Castelfranco Veneto, 1477/1478 - Venice, 1510)

1. *Portrait of Laura* (1506). Vienna, Kunsthistorisches Museum.

2. *Portrait of an Old Woman* (1508-1510). Venice, Gallerie dell'Accademia.

3. *The Three Philosophers* (c. 1508). Vienna, Kunsthistorisches Museum.

1

2

3

Michelangelo

Against the will of his father Ludovico Buonarroti, podesta of Chiusi and Caprese, Michelangelo entered Ghirlandaio's *bottega* in Florence in 1488. Shortly afterwards he was taken under the wing of Lorenzo de' Medici, who sponsored talented young artists, and had access to the Medicean garden of San Marco. After having completed some early works, Michelangelo went to Rome, where in 1501 he sculpted the *Pietà* (Vatican City, Saint Peter's Basilica). When he returned to Florence he painted the *Doni Tondo* (Florence, Uffizi) and sculpted his *David* (Florence, Accademia). In 1505, he was invited to Rome by Pope Julius II, who commissioned Michelangelo to sculpt his funeral monument (Rome, San Pietro in Vincoli); there thus began the "tragedy of the tomb" that came to an end only in 1545 after a seemingly unending series of delusions and interruptions. In 1508, Michelangelo signed the contract for the ceiling frescoes of the Sistine Chapel. In 1513 he again took up work in Florence, in particular the plans for San Lorenzo: he designed a facade (which never materialized) for the church, the new sacristy, and the Laurentian Library for the Medicis. He left Florence forever in 1534 to return to Rome, where until 1541 he was engaged in frescoing the *Last Judgement* in the Sistine Chapel. Afterwards, Michelangelo dedicated most of his time to architectural projects, including renovation Piazza del Campidoglio and the raising of the dome of Saint Peter's. Until the very end of his life he explored the variations of a theme dear to his heart, the *Pietà*, and expressed his reflections in sculpture (Florence, Opera del Duomo; Milan, Castello Sforzesco).

Michelangelo Buonarroti (Caprese, 1475 - Rome, 1564)

1. *The Doni Tondo* (1507). Florence, Uffizi.

2. *Pietà* (1497-1500). Vatican City, Saint Peter's Basilica.

3. *Dying Slave* (1513-1514). Paris, Louvre.

4. *Tomb of Giuliano de' Medici, duc de Nemours,* with *Day* and *Night* (c. 1526-1534). Florence, San Lorenzo, Medici Chapel.

1

2

3

4

Titian

Titian got his start in painting under Giovanni Bellini and later collaborated with Giorgione. Following works on profane and allegorical subjects, such as *Sacred and Profane Love* dated about 1515 (Rome, Galleria Borghese), Titian became the most representative painter of the Venetian Republic. The *Assumption* for the altar of Santa Maria Gloriosa dei Frari (1518), was Titian's first important public commission. During the course of his intense career Titian painted momentous altarpieces (*the Pesaro Altarpiece*, 1519-1526, Venice, Santa Maria dei Frari) but also mythological subjects and portraits. In 1529 and 1530 he was in Bologna, where he painted a portrait of the Holy Roman emperor Charles V (Madrid, Prado), who in 1533 elevated him to the rank of Knight Palatine. From the 1530s through the 1530s he worked for the courts of Mantua, Ferrara and Urbino.

Beginning in about 1540, under the influence of central and northern Italian Mannerism, a change in Titian's manner also became apparent. In 1545-1546 he was in Rome, where he received Roman citizenship and painted the portrait of *Paul III with his Nephews* (Naples, Museo di Capodimonte). In 1548, he went to Augsburg, from whence he returned only in 1551 after having painted the equestrian portrait of *Charles V at the Battle of Mühlberg* (Madrid, Prado). Among his most devoted patrons was the future Philip II of Spain. A further shift in Titian's style, toward what has been defined as "magical impressionism," came in about 1558.

Tiziano Vecellio (Pieve di Cadore, c. 1490 - Venice, 1576)

1. *Young Man with Cap and Gloves* (c. 1520-1525). Paris, Louvre.

2. *Madonna with Saints and Members of the Pesaro Family* (1519-1520). Venice, Santa Maria Gloriosa dei Frari.

3. *Sacred and Profane Love* (1515). Rome, Galleria Borghese.

1

2

3

The Cupola of Santa Maria del Fiore

In 1418, Filippo Brunelleschi and other artists of the time participated in a competition held by the Opera del Duomo for the cupola of the Santa Maria del Fiore cathedral. Given the enormous width of the span, Brunelleschi daringly proposed to build the dome without the aid of formwork (that is, without making use of the centering timbers that had previously been considered absolutely necessary), and submitted his model. Following lengthy consultation, on 16 April 1420 the task of building the cupola was entrusted to Brunelleschi, but jointly with Ghiberti. Brunelleschi thus pretended to take ill; when it became apparent that without his collaboration Ghiberti was unable to proceed profitably, the job became his alone. Brunelleschi's cupola consists of two layers, an inner dome spanning the diameter and a concentric outer shell; the space between the two domes, which is still practicable, contains a sort of skeleton reminiscent of the interlaced meridians and parallels on a globe. The construction is topped by a lantern, also designed by Brunelleschi. In 1486, a golden globe was added at the summit. Brunelleschi, in order to guarantee the success of the work, organized his construction site like any modern builder: at the beginning he hired only masons from Lombardia, less liable to strike than were the Florentine workmen; he had "snack bars" installed on the scaffolding, where bread and wine were sold; he installed a lighting system in the space between the two shells; he personally supervised the work of the carpenters, smiths, and stone-cutters; and he designed the machinery most suitable for every task and occasion.

1. Axonometric projection of the cupola of Santa Maria del Fiore.

2. Filippo Brunelleschi, the cupola of Santa Maria del Fiore (1418-1436). Florence. View of exterior with the walkway begun by Baccio d'Agnolo in 1502 and abandoned due in part to criticism from Michelangelo.

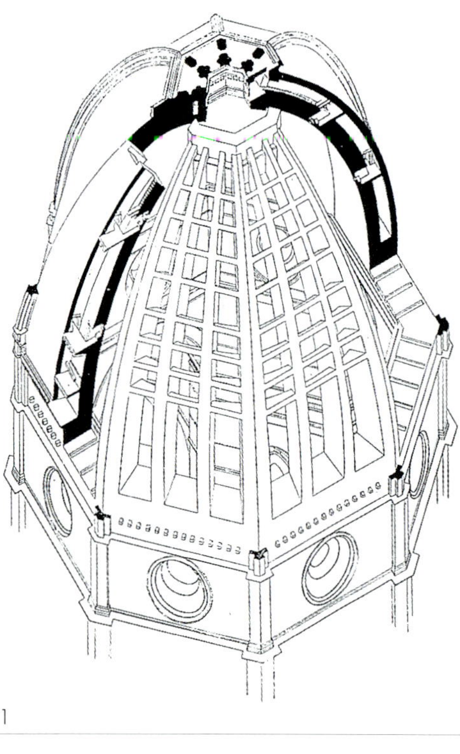

1

2

The Brancacci Chapel Frescoes

It was probably Felice Brancacci who commissioned Masolino to paint the *Scenes from the Life of Saint Peter* in honor of his uncle Piero, the founder of the chapel in Florence's Santa Maria del Carmine church. Masolino began the work in 1424, and shortly thereafter called in Masaccio as his assistant. When Masolino left for Hungary in September, Masaccio was left to continue the work on his own, but he left it unfinished when he left for Rome in 1427. Meanwhile, Felice Brancacci had been exiled (1435) and declared a rebel (1458), and the frescoes remained unfinished. In 1460, the friars placed the 13th-century *Madonna del Popolo* on the altar, leaning against the back wall, perhaps canceling out the *Crucifixion of Saint Peter* painted there. Between 1480 and 1485 the friars asked Filippino Lippi, son of Fra' Filippo Lippi, a painter himself and a former member of that monastery, to complete the opus. The overpaintings in the seventeenth and eighteenth centuries that destroyed the frescoes of the vault and the lunettes, the fire of 1771, and invasive "restoration" actions of the early twentieth century had completely transfigured this important chapter in Florentine art. Recent restoration work, however, has proven the truth of the words of Valery in his *Voyage en Italie* of 1836: "A few feet of wall painted *a fresco* will make the Carmine church live forever in the annals of art."

1. Masaccio and Filippino Lippi, *Resurrection of the Child* and *Saint Peter Enthroned* (1424.-1427). Florence, Santa Maria del Carmine, Brancacci Chapel.

2. Masaccio, *The Expulsion of Adam and Eve from Paradise.*

3. Masolino, *Adam and Eve in Paradise.*

1

2

3

David in Florentine sculpture

The biblical hero who slew the giant Goliath was an oft-portrayed subject in the Florentine Quattrocento. Early in the century, Donatello sculpted the marble *David* (Florence, Bargello) that in 1416 was purchased by the Signoria and placed in Palazzo Vecchio. By 1408, Donatello had sculpted another *David* for the series of the *Prophets* destined to be stand on the on the buttresses of the cathedral; the work has been lost. But the artist's masterpiece is the bronze *David* (Florence, Bargello) mentioned in a chronicle of the times as having been placed in the courtyard of Palazzo Medici in 1469 on occasion of the wedding of Lorenzo il Magnifico and Clarice Orsini. In 1494, after the expulsion of the Medicis from Florence, the work was confiscated by the new republican government and installed in the courtyard of Palazzo della Signoria. The Medici family commissioned Verrocchio to make another bronze *David* (Florence, Bargello), but this too was moved to the public building, having been sold in 1476 by Lorenzo il Magnifico to the Signoria. Between 1502 and 1504, still under the republican government, Michelangelo sculpted his famous marble *David*, which may have been originally destined for the *Prophets* series for the cathedral. But even before the work was completed it had been decided that it would stand in front of the public palace: portrayed without the head of Goliath at his feet, still awaiting his meeting with his enemy, the powerful, proud youth was the eternal sentinel standing in defense of the republican liberties.

1. Donatello, *David* (1440-1443), bronze. Florence, Bargello.

2. Donatello, *David* (1412), marble. Florence, Bargello.

3. Verrocchio, *David* (c. 1475). Florence, Bargello.

4. Michelangelo, *David* (1504). Florence, Accademia.

1

2

3

4

The Gates of Paradise

The east portal of the Florentine Baptistery, that facing the facade of the cathedral, is called the "Golden Door" in honor of its splendid mercury-amalgam gilding, or the "Gates of Paradise" after a well-known exclamation proffered by Michelangelo.

The work in bronze, representing episodes from the Old Testament, was commissioned of Ghiberti in 1425, when the artist has just finished the pair of doors now on the north side of the building. The work was sponsored by the Arte della Calimala, and the consultant for the iconographic layout was the chancellor of the Florentine Republic, Leonardo Bruni. But Ghiberti decided on a structure which although still showing much Gothic influence was very different from that of the earlier north portals: he designed ten great quadrangular panels, depicting thirty-seven episodes in all, each in sweeping perspective. The scenes are constructed using full-round modeling in the foreground that flattens out more and more as the design recedes toward the background, as Donatello had done in *Saint George and the Dragon* (Florence, Bargello).

Each wing of the door is framed by twenty-four niches with full figures of biblical characters alternating with the same number of tondi with heads in relief. Among these are a self-portrait of Ghiberti with his son Vittorio. And the signature is legible in a cornice: "Laurentii Cionis de Ghibertis. Mira arte fabricatum."

Today a copy stands in the place of the original portal, which is undergoing restoration and upon completion will be exhibited in the Museo dell'Opera del Duomo.

1. Lorenzo Ghiberti, one of the oculi on the jambs of the *Gates of Paradise*; may be a self-portrait of the artist.

2. Lorenzo Ghiberti, *Gates of Paradise* (1425-1452). Florence, Baptistery, prior to replacement of the original with a copy.

3. Lorenzo Ghiberti, *Scenes from the Life of Abraham*, from the *Gates of Paradise*. Florence. Museo dell'Opera del Duomo (formerly installed on the Baptistery).

4. Lorenzo Ghiberti, *The Meeting of Solomon and the Queen of Sheba*, from the *Gates of Paradise*.

1

2

3

4

The Facade of Santa Maria Novella

In 1456, Giovanni di Paolo Rucellai ordered Leon Battista Alberti to make, or it might better be said to complete, the facade of the church of Santa Maria Novella in Florence. The side portals had been hung and the ogival arcatures set in the Trecento, and the wheel window had already been opened above. The difficulty lay in creating a work capable of integrating the preexisting parts and at the same time reflecting the modern Renaissance prerogatives, and in particular the principles of harmony and beauty. The facade is based on modular relationships that link the single parts, using the square as the basic module. The marble intarsia, white and green as Gothic tradition would have it, create designs that refer back to a complex iconological program. The emblem of Giovanni Rucellai, the sail of fortune filed by the wind, the family emblem of, feathers inserted in a ring, recurs in the cornice of the window. The name of the patron and the date of completion of the work, 1470, are inscribed on high in cubital letters in the frieze underneath the tympanum, which in turn is dominated by the sunburst that is the symbol of the Dominican order. For Rucellai, Alberti also designed the palace in Via della Vigna, the garden and the front loggia of the palace, and the chapel annexed to the nearby church of San Pancrazio, with the small temple of the Holy Sepulchre in its interior.

1. Leon Battista Alberti, facade of Santa Maria Novella (1456). Florence.

2. Detail of the tympanum and the wheel window.

3. Detail of a scroll.

1

2

3

The Flagellation

"Opus Petri de Burgo Sci Sepulcri" (Work by Piero di Borgo San Sepolcro). This is the signature of the author – Piero della Francesca – that we read on Pilate's seat in the mysterious *Flagellation* of Urbino. The theory had been advanced that the work alluded to events regarding Federico da Montefeltro, Piero's most important patron, but more recent hypotheses are that the scene refers to the fall of Constantinople in 1453; the flagellated Christ would represent the Church, "martyred" by the infidel; the three figures in the right foreground would be discussing the crusade requested by Pope Pius II at the Council of Mantua in 1459. Of the three figures, the identities of two are dubious. That dressed in blue and gold brocade, instead, is certainly Giovanni Bacci, who in 1452 commissioned Piero to paint the frescoes of the *Legend of the True Cross* in the church of San Francesco in Arezzo. Bacci was an official of the papal curia and a fervent supporter of reconciliation between the Eastern and Western Churches. In the Aretine frescoes, Bacci wanted a reference to the crusade launched against the Turks, and requested that Piero emphasize two battle scenes: The *Victory of Constantine over Maxentius* and the *Battle between Heraclius and Chosroes*, both represented in the lower register of the chapel; the second portrays Bacci in left profile among the onlookers on the right.

1. Piero della Francesca, *The Flagellation* (c. 1460). Urbino, Galleria Nazionale delle Marche.

2. Detail of the background scene.

1

2

The Frescoes of the Collegio del Cambio

The Collegio del Cambio in the Palazzo Comunale of Perugia is decorated with a precious cycle of frescoes by Pietro Perugino, founder of the Umbrian school and the most sought-after artist at the papal court before the arrival of Raphael and Michelangelo. The tasks performed by the Collegio del Cambio (the bankers' guild) included money-changing, works of charity, and issuing judgements in cases regarding pecuniary disputes. The hearings were held in the Sala dell'Udienza, with its carved wooden bench or "tribunal." On 26 January 1496, the Collegio decided to entrust the pictorial decoration to Pietro Perugino, who in that period was extremely busy with his two studios, one in Perugia and one in Florence. The artist followed the iconographic program dictated by the humanist Francesco Maturanzio. The ceiling, divided into in vaulting cells by elegant ribs, is richly decorated with grotesques and tondi, each containing the representation of a *Planet*; the planets are dominated by *Apollo* in the largest tondo in the central lozenge. On the left side wall are groups of *Famous Men* with the *Virtues*; on the right, *Prophets and Sibyls* accompanied by the *Eternal Father in Glory*. On the end wall are the *Transfiguration* and the *Nativity* of Christ. Pagan civilization finds a meeting point with Christian culture in the figure of the Christ: the former is the anticipation of the latter, which is its Revelation.

1. Perugino, frescoes in the Sala dell'Udienza of the Collegio del Cambio (1496-1500). Perugia.

2. Perugino, detail of the *Famous Men* with the Virtues. Perugia, Collegio del Cambio.

3. Perugino, *Self-Portrait*. Perugia, Collegio del Cambio.

1

2

3

Primavera

As soon as it was completed, in 1481-1482, Botticelli's *Primavera* (*The Spring*) was transported to the Florentine palace of Lorenzo di Pierfrancesco de' Medici, second cousin of il Magnifico, and hung in the antechamber above the back of a "daybed", in reality a precious chest. As complex as interpretation of the subject might seem, the characters have by now been positively identified. The scene is set in an ideal garden with an orange grove and a lawn with dozens of different varieties of flowers. The painting reads from right to left. Zephyr, the western wind that announces the coming of Spring, captures Chloris, a nymph of the garden of the Hesperides, and possesses her. Chloris, as Zephyr's bride, receives the gift of the power to make every flowering species bud, and is transformed into the goddess Flora, the personification of a fertile and generous Nature. The garden is dominated by Venus standing against bush of myrtle, the symbol of Humanitas; that is, of the harmonious interpenetration of Man's spiritual and intellectual activities. The goddess is accompanied by a blindfolded Cupid who hurls his dart in the direction of the three Graces while they are performing a circular dance, holding hands with their fingers intertwined, representing "liberality" (Alberti), which is given by one, received by another, and returned by the third. On the far left is Mercury, the messenger of the gods in winged boots, who with the caduceus banishes the clouds from the garden.

1. Botticelli. *Primavera* (1481-1482), detail of the figure of Flora. Florence, Uffizi.

2. Detail of the three Graces.

3. Botticelli, *La Primavera*. Florence, Uffizi.

1

2

3

The Wedding Chamber

In 1474, Andrea Mantegna completed the decoration of the room on the *piano nobile* of the north tower of the castle of San Giorgio in Mantua. The intention was that of celebrating the Gonzaga family, the lords of the city and the patrons of the artist. Improperly called the "Wedding Chamber" in modern times, the room was actually designed for entertainment functions and housed the private archives of Ludovico Gonzaga.

The "newlyweds" recalled in a dedicatory plaque over a door are the abovementioned Ludovico and his wife Barbara of Brandenburg, portrayed surrounded by their children and the dignitaries above the fireplace, in an illusionistic open-air portico. Like in a group photograph, all are in an official pose, to the exception of Ludovico, who is distracted by an important letter delivered by his secretary Marsilio Andreasi: it is the official announcement of the appointment of Ludovico's son Francesco as cardinal, a fundamental event in the politics of the marquess of Mantua and a recurring motif in the pictorial cycle.

The total spatial illusion cycle concludes with the homogeneous decoration of the ceiling, with the emblems of the Gonzaga house, mythological scenes, portraits of Roman emperors, and, at the center, an oculus or circular opening to the sky, with daring *sotto in su* putti and figures looking into the room around a balustrade with a peacock and a vase, all in dramatically foreshortened perspective. This is doubtless the most influential illusionistic perspective invention of the Italian Quattrocento.

1. Andrea Mantegna, *Meeting of Ludovico Gonzaga with the Cardinal Francesco Gonzaga*, from the *Wedding Chamber* (c. 1465 - 1474). Mantua, Castel San Giorgio.

2. *The Gonzaga Papers* from the *Wedding Chamber*.

3. Oculus with putti and figures, ceiling of the *Wedding Chamber*.

1

2

3

The Last Supper

In 1498, after many promptings from the prior, Leonardo completed the *Last Supper* in the monastery of Santa Maria delle Grazie in Milan. In handling this theme, oft-represented in the 15th century in Florence, whence came the artist to Milan, Leonard succeeded in interpreting it in a modern key and in playing up the emotional reactions of the characters. "One of you will betray me," said Christ, and the Apostles, moving into groups of three, immediately express those "movements of the soul," those emotions which were for the master the primary reason for painting to exist. The poor conditions of the work, currently undergoing restoration, are party due to the experimental technique used by the artist, tempera mixed with oil on two layers of plaster, which proved to be much less resistant than traditional fresco. In order to leave time for his experiments, Leonardo worked very slowly: he was often seen going to the refectory only about midday, painting a few brushstrokes, and then leaving the work alone for days on end. But the prior wanted his wall completed, and even asked that Ludovico il Moro be brought in as assistant. Leonardo lost his patience at that and, as he explained to the duke in person (who got a good laugh out of it), took his revenge by using the face of the prelate for Judas, whose features were creating for him as much difficulty as those of Christ. But for the latter figure the master was unable to find an equally suitable model.

1. Leonardo, *The Last Supper*. Detail.

2. Leonardo, *The Last Supper* (1494-1498). Milan, Santa Maria delle Grazie.

3. Ghirlandaio, *The Last Supper* (c. 1480). Florence, San Marco (following restoration).

1

2

3

The Tempest

In the early sixteenth century (the dates proposed vary between 1502 and 1508), Giorgione painted *The Tempest*, a work of extraordinary charm, for his friend Gabriele Vendramin, a habitué of the Venetian intellectual circles. The painting is mentioned as being in Vendramin's "*camerino delle anticaglie*" in 1530 by Marcantonio Michiel, another educated Venetian patrician, who described it as a "little landscape with the tempest [hence today's title] with the gipsy and soldier." Is the painting then just a simple landscape, however enriched by the author's imagination and technique? This is the opinion of some critics, who are nevertheless opposed by a long list of scholars who in the last two centuries have proposed mythological, allegorical, alchemical, biblical and historical readings of the work. But for now the debate is still unresolved, since each hypothesis seems to vacillate when confronted with another.

One thing is certain, and it emerges from the diagnostic studies conducted on the canvas: Giorgione developed the work directly on the canvas, not from a cartoon, and made a number of changes and corrections as he proceeded. X-rays have revealed a nude woman seated in the water in the lower lefthand corner of the work, where the soldier now stands; in place of the two columns there was a tower; the nursing woman once wore a blouse.

1. Giorgione, *The Tempest*, detail of the nursing woman.

2. Giorgione, *The Tempest* (1502-1508). Venice, Gallerie dell'Accademia.

1

2

The Garden of Earthly Delights

During those years in which in Italy the works of Leonardo, Raphael and Michelangelo brought the Renaissance to the high point of its parabola, in Flanders, the oneiric, alchemical visions of Hieronymus Bosch reflected the eternal struggle between Good and Evil in man's difficult journey toward salvation. Voluptuousness is the theme of the unsettling triptych of the *Garden of Earthly Delights*.

Closed, the painting represents the third day of the Creation: the earth is immersed in water and enclosed in a sphere of crystal, the emblem of fragility. The panels open onto the *Garden of Earthly Delights*, where men and women, both Black and White, in couples, by threes, or in groups, share the pleasures of the senses. At the center of the composition the libidinous procession winds around the fountain of youth. In the background, at the center of a pool, is instead the fountain of adultery, in the form of a globe. The entire painting is in interweaving of animal, plant and mineral motifs alluding to erotism, derived from popular tradition, literature and alchemy.

The *Earthly Paradise* of the left panel, showing the meeting of Adam and Eve, is the prelude to the central scene of the *Garden of Earthly Delights*, while the conclusion is found in the horrors of the *Hell* depicted on the right panel, in which the musical instruments – harp, lute and organ – are instruments of torture. At the center of this image is the alchemical man, his legs tree trunks, his body an egg, and his face probably the portrait of Bosch himself.

1. Hieronymus Bosch, *The Earthly Paradise*, left panel of the triptych of *The Garden of Earthly Delights* (1503-1504). Madrid, Prado.

2. Hieronymus Bosch, *Hell*, right panel of the triptych.

3. Hieronymus Bosch, *The Garden of Earthly Delights*, center panel of the triptych.

4. Hieronymus Bosch, *The Earthly Paradise*, detail of the left panel of the triptych.

5. Hieronymus Bosch, *Hell*, detail of the right panel.

1

2

3

4

5

The Room of the Segnatura

As soon as he reached Rome in 1508, Raphael began painting the apartment selected by Julius II in the Vatican Palace, and by 1511 had finished the first of the rooms, called the *Stanza della Segnatura* because it was later the seat of the *Signatura Gratiae* tribunal. The frescoes are allegories of the ideas of Truth, Good and Beauty. Revealed Truth is theology, represented by the *Dispute of the Blessed Sacrament* in which, in the earthly and militant Church, there appear the portraits of Beato Angelico, Bramante, Julius II, Dante and Savonarola. Facing Good is rational Truth, the philosophy of the *School of Athens* with at its center Plato (with Leonardo's countenance) and Aristotle; among the contemporary figures portrayed here, Raphael added Michelangelo at the last minute, perhaps when the ceiling of the Sistine Chapel was uncovered. The artist is depicted alone and pensive, in the role of Heracleitus. Moral good is represented by the *Cardinal Virtues* in the lunette of the intermediate wall, but Good is also that moral good imposed by law, whether the canonical law of *Gregory IX Approving the Decretals* or the civil law of *Tribonian Delivering the Pandects to Justinian*. Beauty is identified with Poetry, which has its apotheosis in the *Parnassus* painted on the facing wall: the poets of the time welcomed by Apollo and the Muses include Dante, Petrarch and Boccaccio.

1. Raphael, *Parnassus* (1508-1511). Rome, Vatican Palace, Room of the Segnatura.

2. Raphael, *The School of Athens* (1508-1511). Rome, Vatican Palace, Room of the Segnatura.

1

2

The Ceiling of the Sistine Chapel

In 1508, when Julius II summoned Raphael to Rome, he also called on Michelangelo, to whom he entrusted the task of frescoing the ceiling of the Sistine chapel with scenes from the *Genesis* and *Sibyls* and *Prophets*, the vaulting cells with biblical scenes predating Moses, and the lunettes with the *Ancestors of Christ*. It is told how the pope was influenced by the architect Bramante, who went to great lengths to create difficulties for Buonarroti, who had never before worked in fresco. Michelangelo refused the job repeatedly, but the impetuous pope was not to be dissuaded. Thus the artist called in some Florentine painters, experts in the art of the *buon fresco*, but as soon as he had mastered the technique he dismissed them summarily and continued his work alone. But he didn't stop there: for months he kept his work hidden, until on 14 August 1511 the pope forced him to remove the scaffolding. All of Rome came to see, including the envious Bramante, who immediately suggested to the pope to charge Raphael, also in Rome at the time, with completion of the work.

But the pope ordered Michelangelo to continue. The artist was perennially discontent with what he had done, and kept requesting extra time until the by this time furious pope ordered him to finish immediately and threatened to personally pull him down from his scaffolding. Thus, by October 1512, Michelangelo completed the ceiling.

He returned to the Sistine chapel in 1535 to fresco the Last Judgement for Pope Paul III.

1. Michelangelo, *Judith and Holophernes*, detail of the ceiling of the Sistine Chapel (1508-1512). Rome, Vatican Palaces.

2. Ceiling and walls of the Sistine Chapel.

3. Michelangelo, *Jonah*.

4. Michelangelo, *The Temptation*.

1

2

3

4

Chronology	1400	1410	1420
Italy	1401. In Florence, competition for the portal of the Baptistery, won by Ghiberti. Birth of Masaccio. 1402. Death of Giangaleazzo Visconti. 1406-1407. Jacopo della Quercia sculpts the Funeral Monument of Ilaria del Carretto for the cathedral of Lucca. 1409. In Venice, Gentile da Fabriano and Pisanello begin the frescoes (now lost) in the ducal palace.	1414. Poggio Bracciolini finds Vitruvius' *De Architettura*. 1415. In Florence, Nanni di Banco sculpts the *Four Crowned Saints* for Orsanmichele in Florence. 1416. Ghiberti completes his *Saint John the Baptist* for Orsanmichele. 1417. *Saint George* by Donatello, for Orsanmichele.	1423. In Florence: *The Adoration of the Magi* by Gentile da Fabriano for Santa Trinita; Brunelleschi take over construction of the cupola. 1424-1428. Masolino and Masaccio fresco the Brancacci Chapel in Santa Maria del Carmine. 1428. Death of Masaccio in Rome. In Florence, Brunelleschi completes the Old Sacristy in San Lorenzo.
Low Countries	1402. Pol and Jehannequin Limbourg enter the service of Philip the Bold, duke of Burgundy.	1419-1467. Reign of Philip the Good, duke of Burgundy; the annexation of the Flemish provinces to the duchy of Burgundy, begun under Philip the Bold, is completed. The court moves to Bruges.	1425. University opened in Louvain. Jan van Eyck is appointed *valet de chambre* at the court of Philip III (the Good) of Burgundy. 1427-1428. In Tournai, the Master of Flémalle (perhaps Robert Campin) paints the Triptych of Merode.
France	1402. With the tapestries for the cathedral of Tournai, the fame of the Arras weavers surpasses that of the French. 1406. Claus Sluter dies in Dijon.	1413-1416. The Limbourg brothers decorate the illuminated manuscript *Très riches heures* (Chantilly, Musée Condé) for Jean duke of Berry. 1415. French defeated at Azincourt in the Thirty Years' War. 1418-1425. Miniatures of the *Heures de Rohan* for Jolanda of Aragon, wife of Louis II d'Anjou.	1420. Treaty of Troyes. 1422-1461. Reign of Charles VI the Victorious.
England		1413-1422. Reign of Henry V. 1415. Victory over the French at Azincourt.	
Spain, Germany and the rest of Europe	1401. Construction of the new cathedral begins in Seville.	1412. Ferdinando I becomes king of Aragon.	

1430	1440	1450	1460
1434. Cosimo de' Medici returns to Florence from exile. Revolt against papal rule. Eugenius IV goes to Florence. 1435. Beginning of the struggle between Renato d'Angiò and Alfonso IV of Aragon for succession to the throne of the Kingdom of Naples. 1436. Leon Battista Alberti writes *De Pictura*. Pope Eugenius IV consecrates the cupola of the Florence cathedral.	1439-1445. In Florence, Beato Angelico frescoes the Monastery of San Marco. 1442. Alfonso of Aragon ascends the throne of the Kingdom of Naples; imports works by van Eyck and van der Weyden. The Florentine Andrea del Castagno is in Venice. 1443. Donatello sets out for Padua. 1444. In Florence, Michelozzo begins Palazzo Medici-Riccardi.	1450. In Rome, Jubilee proclaimed by Pope Nicholas V. Francesco Sforza enters Milan and proclaims himself duke. 1454. Treaty of Lodi and constitution of the Italic League. 1458. Enea Silvio Piccolomini is elected Pope Pius II. 1459. Bernardo Rossellino begins drawing his plans for Pienza.	1460. Alberti and Mantegna are in Mantua. 1460-1465. In Milan, Filarete designs the ideal city of Sforzinda for Francesco Sforza. 1466. In Urbino, Luciano Laurana continues work on the ducal palace. In Naples, the *Arch of Triumph* of Alfonso of Aragon is erected. 1469-1470. Frescoes in Palazzo Schifanoia in Ferrara.
1430-1432. *Triptych of Flémalle* (Frankfurt, Städelsches Kunstinstitut). 1432. Jan van Eyck completes the polyptych for the altar of Saint-Bavon in Ghent. 1434. Jan van Eyck paints the portrait of *Giovanni Arnolfini and his Wife*. 1435 (c.). In Tournai, Rogier van der Weyden paints the *Deposition* (Madrid, Prado).	1443-1451. Nicolas Rolin, chancellor to Philip the Good, commissions the Rogier van der Weyden to paint the polyptych of the *Last Judgement* for the hospital of Beaune.	1450. van der Weyden goes to Rome for the Jubilee and stops in Florence. 1455 (c.). In tapestry-making, the Arras workshops decline and those of Tournai develop.	1464-1467. Dirck Bouts paints the polyptych of the *Last Supper* for the church of Saint Pierre in Louvain.
1431. Joan of Arc is burned at the stake for heresy and witchcraft. 1435. Treaty of Arras between Philip III the Good, duke of Burgundy, and Charles VII. Renato d'Angiò, king of Naples, is prisoner in Dijon. At about this time, Nicolas Rolin donates the *Madonna of the Chancellor* by Jan van Eyck (Paris, Louvre) to the Autun cathedral.	1442. The altarpiece of the *Annunciation* is commissioned for the church of Saint-Saveur in Aix-en-Provence. 1445. Choir of Mont-Saint-Michel. 1448 (c.). Stained-glass window of the *Annunciation* for the cathedral of Bourges. Jean Fouquet begins the miniatures of the *Book of Hours* for Étienne Chevalier, minister to Charles VII.	1453. Battle of Castillon. The Guienna is retaken. End of the Hundred Years' War. 1453-1464. *Coronation of the Virgin* by Enguerrand Charonton (Villeneuve-les-Avignon, Musée).	1460 (c.). Facade of the cathedral of Tours in "flamboyant Gothic" style. 1461-1483. Reign of Louis XI.
	1441. Henry VI founds King's College in Cambridge. 1446. Start of construction of the chapel in the courtyard of King's College; completed in 1515.	1453. End of the Hundred Years' War: the English are cast out of all French territory except Calais. 1455-1485. War of the Roses between the families of York and Lancaster.	
1431. The Spanish painter Louis Dalmau meets Jan van Eyck in Bruges 1432. Lukas Moser paints the Magdalen altarpiece for the church of Tiefenbronn. 1438-1439. In Germany, reign of Albrecht II of Austria: the crown definitively passes to the Hapsburgs.	1442. Alfonso V king of Aragon becomes king of Naples, Sicily and Sardinia. 1442-1444. Paintings by Stefan Lochner for the high altar of the cathedral. 1444. *The Miraculous Draught of Fishes* by Konrad Witz in Geneva. 1445. *The Virgin of the Councillors* by Luis Dalmau in Barcelona.	1450. Invention of printing. 1453. The Turks conquer Constantinople. 1455. In Mainz, Gutenberg publishes the *Bible*.	1469. Marriage of Isabella, heiress to Castle and Ferdinando heir to Aragon.

Chronology

	1470	1480	1490
Italy	1474. In Mantua, Mantegna completes the *Wedding Chamber* frescoes. 1475. Justus of Ghent is at the court of Urbino. 1476. Gian Galeazzo Sforza is duke of Milan, first under the regency of his mother Bona of Savoy and then (1480) under his uncle Ludovico il Moro. 1477. Bramante is in Milan. 1478. Florence: Pazzi family plot against the Medicis.	1481-1482. Sixtus IV calls Cosimo Rosselli, Botticelli, Ghirlandaio, Perugino and Signorelli to paint the Sistine Chapel. 1482-1484. War of Ferrara. 1482 (c.). Botticelli paints the *Birth of Venus* and *La Primavera*. Leonardo leaves for Milan. 1483. The *Portinari Triptych* (Uffizi) by Hugo van der Goes is brought to Florence from Bruges for Sant'Egidio.	1492. In Milan, Bramante completes the choir of Santa Maria delle Grazie. Lorenzo il Magnifico dies in Florence. In Rome, election of Pope Alexander VI Borgia. 1494. Charles VIII invades Italy. The Medicis are driven out of Florence and the Republic is proclaimed. 1499. Milan is occupied by Louis XII of France; Leonardo and Bramante leave the city.
Low Countries	1477. Death of Charles the Bold, the last Duke of Burgundy; accentuation of the conflicts between the Hapsburgs and the Valois' for possession of the Low Countries. Maria, daughter of Charles the Bold, marries Maximilian of Austria.	1482. Death of Maria of Burgundy. 1482-1506. Philip the Handsome of Hapsburg, son of Maximilian, becomes prince of the Low Countries.	
France	1475. Peace of Picquigny; Louis XI limits England's right of possession in French territory to Calais alone. 1477. Louis XI unites all French territory, including Burgundy and Provence.	1483-1498. Reign of Charles VIII, who lays claim to Naples.	1491. Charles VIII marries Anne of Brittany. 1494-1495. Charles VIII invades Italy, claiming the kingdom of Naples, but retreats following defeat at the hands of the league composed of Spain, Hapsburg and the Italian states. 1498-1515. Reign of Louis XII, who as heir of the Viscontis lays claim to the duchy of Milan. 1498-1500. Triptych of the *Madonna with Saints and Donors* for the cathedral of Moulins.
England	1476. W. Caxton introduces printing in England.	1485-1509. Reign of Henry VII Tudor, supported by the Lancasters.	1490. Construction of the Oxford Divinity School completed. 1492-1509. Construction of the bell tower for the facade of Magdalen College, Oxford. 1493-1505. The center tower of the Canterbury Cathedral (Bell Harry) is built in perpendicular Gothic style.
Spain, Germany and the rest of Europe	1470-1480. The Spanish painter Pédro Berruguete is in Italy. 1473. In Colmar (Alsace), Schongauer paints the *Madonna in the Rose Garden* for San Martin's church. 1474. Isabella I of Castile ascends the throne. 1477. Maximilian of Hapsburg marries Maria of Burgundy. 1478. Ferdinando and Isabella reinstate the Inquisition.	1481. Michael Pacher carves and paints the altarpiece for the church of Saint Wolfgang in Salzburg.	1492. Conquest of Granada. Christopher Columbus discovers America. 1493. Maximilian of Hapsburg becomes emperor. 1494. Marriage of Philip the Handsome of Hapsburg to the infanta of Spain Juana the Mad. 1498. Dürer produces his *Apocalypse* series of woodcuts. 1499. Treaty of Basel.

1500	1510	1520	1530
1503. Election of Pope Julius II. 1504-1506. In Florence, Leonardo and Michelangelo prepare the cartoons for the *Battles* for Palazzo della Signoria. Raphael is in Florence. In Venice, Giorgione and Titian fresco the Fondaco dei Tedeschi. In Rome, Michelangelo begins the ceiling of the Sistine Chapel and Raphael the Room of the Segnatura.	1511. The Holy League opposes Louis XII. 1512. The Medicis return to Florence. The Sforzas return to power in Milan with Maximilian. 1513. Election of Pope Leo X. 1515. Francis I king of France conquers the duchy of Milan. Machiavelli writes *The Prince*. 1516. Ludovico Ariosto publishes *Orlando Furioso*.	1520. *Exurge Domine*, papal bull against Luther. Death of Raphael. 1520-1530. In Parma, Correggio frescoes the cupolas of San Giovanni and of the cathedral. 1523. Election of Pope Clement VII. 1525. In Pavia, Francis I is defeated by Charles V. 1527. Sack of Rome; diaspora of the artists. The last Republic is proclaimed in Florence.	1530. Titian paints his first portrait of Charles V (now lost) in Bologna. Rosso Fiorentino is in France. 1536. Michelangelo begins the *Last Judgement* in the Sistine Chapel.
1500. On 24 February Charles of Hapsburg, the future Charles V, is born in Ghent. 1503-1504. In Bois-le-Duc, Bosch paints the triptych of the *Garden of Earthly Delights*. 1506. Charles of Hapsburg becomes prince of the Low Countries. The *Madonna with Child* sculpted by Michelangelo for the church of Notre-Dame comes to Bruges.	1511. Gérard David paints the *Wedding of Saint Catherine*. Erasmus of Rotterdam publishes the *Praise of Folly*. 1518. Bernaert van Orley is named court painter. 1519. Pieter van Aelst, Brussels' most important weaver, makes the tapestries with the *Acts of the Apostles* after Raphael's cartoons (Rome, Pinacoteca Vaticana).	1520. Lucas van Leyden paints the triptych of the *Last Judgement*. 1520-1521. In Antwerp, Dürer meets Joachim Patinir.	
1504. Treaty of Lyon: Naples ceded to Spain, Milan to France. 1500-1505. Jean Perréal paints the portrait of *Pierre Sala*; as court painter, visits Italy repeatedly until 1509. 1501. Start of construction of the chateau of cardinal Georges d'Amboise in Gaillon, in Normandy.	1512. Louis XII, defeated by the Holy League, withdraws from Milan. 1515-1547. Reign of Francis I. 1515. Victory of Francis I at Marignano. 1516. In Bologna, pact with Leo X, in Freiburg with the Swiss and in Noyon with Spain. 1519. Leonardo dies on 2 May in the Cloux chateau near Amboise. Work begins on the Chambord chateau.	1521. Francis I opens the Franco-Hapsburg conflict, closed only in 1559. 1523. Jean Clouet is nominated court painter. 1525. Francis I is defeated at Pavia. 1526. Treaty of Madrid. League of Cognac. 1528. Reconstruction of Fontainebleau begins. 1529. Treaty of Cambrai between France and Spain: Francis I abandons his plans to take Italy.	
1503. Robert and William Vertue begin construction of the chapel of Henry VII in Westminster Abbey. 1509-1547. Reign of Henry VIII.	1511. Henry VIII joins the Holy League. 1512-1518. The Florentine Pietro Torrigiani sculpts the tomb of Henry VII and his wife Elizabeth of York for the apsidal chapel in Westminster Abbey. 1514-1520. The Hampton Court castle is built.	1523-1524. Campaign against France. 1526-1527. While in England, Hans Holbein the Younger paints the *Family of Thomas More*.	
1500. Treaty of Granada between Louis XII and Ferdinando II, who occupies Naples. 1505. Lucas Cranach becomes court painter to the Saxon Elector Friedrich. 1508. Spain joins the League of Cambrai.	1511. Spain joins the Holy League against France. 1516. Charles of Hapsburg becomes king of Spain. Grünewald completes the polyptych in Isenheim. 1517. Martin Luther posts his *95 Theses* to the door of the Wittenberg cathedral. 1518. Hans Holbein the Younger may have traveled to Italy. 1519. Charles of Hapsburg becomes with the name of Charles V. emperor.	1520. Luther burns the bull of excommunication in Wittenberg. 1524. Peasants' War in Germany; Grünewald, in Mainz, participates in insurrections. 1526. Treaty of Madrid. Dürer donates the *Four Apostles* to Nuremberg. 1529. Treaty of Cambrai. Treaty of Barcelona. In Wittenberg, Lucas van Leyden takes Luther as inspiration for his engravings.	1530. Charles V is crowned emperor and king of Italy by Clement VII, in Bologna. Death of Albrecht Dürer.

A Glossary of Renaissance Technique

Drawing. This technique enjoyed extensive development from the late 15th century onward, especially in Florence. The drawing on paper of variable thickness was made in **metal point,** in red or black **pencil**, in **charcoal**, or in **pen**. The drawing was transferred from the **cartoon** to the painting support using one of two techniques: **pouncing** with powdered carbon which passed through perforations along the outlines, or **tracing** the outlines with a point.

Engraving. The development of artistic engraving is linked to the invention of printing and the illustrated book. Among the earliest types of engraving was **line engraving**, practiced the early 15th century in Germany and Flanders and shortly thereafter in Italy in the goldsmiths' studios. This is a "cutaway" type of metal print plate, usually copper, engraved with a truncated point called a burin. Among the most famous artists who used this technique were Martin Schongauer in Germany, Maso Finiguerra in Florence and Andrea Mantegna in the Veneto region. The **drypoint** method was at times used to integrate the burin technique and later on various etching processes were also used. The drypoint technique consists in using a steel or diamond tip to cut finer and more precise lines.

Intarsia. A panel of wood or marble that is cut in accordance with a given pattern and inlaid with differently-colored pieces of the same material to form a design, somewhat like mosaic. The technique was used above all for the facades of the churches (e.g. that of Santa Maria Novella in Florence, by Leon Battista Alberti) and as wall coverings for interiors (e.g., the Studiolo of Federico di Montefeltro in Urbino).

Miniature. From the Latin *minium*, the red pigment used for the first letter of a page, this is the art of decorating manuscripts and parchments with tiny, brightly-colored paintings in the watercolor, enamel or oil mediums. With the development of the printed illustrated book, miniature fell into disuse until practically disappearing in the 16th century.

Mosaic. This ancient technique, consisting in the placement of colored tesserae of different materials to form a design, was still in use in Venice in the 15th century. Under Lorenzo il Magnifico it returned to vogue in Florence and was practiced by Ghirlandaio's workshop.

Painting. The Renaissance inherited the arts of fresco and panel painting from the Giotto and the artistic culture of the 14th century. What changed as regards **fresco** were the design transfer techniques: the *sinopia* (preliminary sketch painted in red ochre) on the first layer of plaster (*arriccio*) disappeared when the technique of **pouncing** or **tracing** the cartoon (cf. **Drawing**) on the second, smoother layer (*tonachino*) came into use. Painting was done on the *tonachino* while it was still fresh, from the top down, on areas of fresh plaster sufficient for a day's work. The colors were pigments diluted in water. The fresco technique was often integrated, or more rarely replaced, by *a secco* painting with tempera on dry plaster. This "vile practice" (Vasari) often resulted in parts of the painting flaking off. **Tempera** was the most widely-used pictorial medium on wood, canvas, stone, metal. and paper supports until the late 15th century, when it was replaced by oil-based paints. Tempera was prepared using pigments dissolved in water and thickened with egg, milk, organic gums, natural glues or other substances thinned with water. Egg tempera, the so-called **tempera grassa** used by Piero della Francesca, Antonello da Messina and Giovanni Bellini, marked the first step toward the brilliance of **oil painting** popularized by the Flemish painters and characterized by pigments ground in fatty plant oils such as linseed, walnut and poppy oils. Another innovation was in the support used for non-mural paintings: the **panel**, usually of poplar wood, was gradually replaced by the **canvas**. In Venice, where the walls were easily damaged by the damp, paintings on canvas replaced even the frescoes: Vittorio Carpaccio's great cycles of paintings amply demonstrate.

Sculpture. Sculpture in stone, preferred for outdoor applications, and wooden sculpture, more suitable for interiors, continued from the Gothic through the Renaissance period. The limestones, the sandstones, the granites, and finally marble, considered a particularly noble and precious medium, were among the most-used materials for **stone sculpture**. The different stages in the working of marble (rough-hewing, smoothing, polishing) are easy to identify in the unfinished works of Michelangelo (e.g., the *Prigioni*; Florence, Accademia). **Wooden sculpture** was generally considered to be a commoner and inferior genre with respect to bronze or marble sculpture. The wood might be varnished (Germany, Flanders), or painted with tempera and gilded. In the latter case, a sheet of linen was first glued onto the wooden surface and then covered with a layer of plaster and glue (e.g., the *Magdalen* by Donatello; Florence, Museo dell'Opera del Duomo). It was in Florence, with Brunelleschi, Ghiberti, Donatello that the techniques of classical antiquity were discovered anew and perfected. Among these, the most important were bronze-casting and terracotta sculpture. **Bronze** is an alloy of copper and a variable, although always lesser, percentage of tin. It is a material that is workable cold, by hammering on sheets of the metal, or hot, by founding and casting, usually by the *cire perdue* hollow-casting process. As regards **terracotta**, it must be mentioned that Luca Della Robbia invented a peculiar genre of sculpture: **glazed terracotta**. The clay sculpture was painted with an enamel similar to that used for maiolica with a siliceous component.

Stained glass. The point of departure for stained-glass windows is a 1:1 scale drawing on cardboard; the pieces of glass are cut to match. The diamond point came into use in the 15th century. The windows of the cathedrals of Florence and Milan and those of All Souls College in Oxford are particularly excellent examples of this technique.

Tapestry. Heavy, patterned or figured handwoven textiles produced using variable techniques and materials, usually fine wool, silk, gold and silver. In Renaissance times, the tapestry-weaver generally based his work on cartoons painted by famous artists such as Raphael (London, Victoria and Albert Museum).

Woodcut or **xylography** is an relief printing procedure that makes use of a slab of hardwood as the plate. The borders inside and outside the outline previously drawn on the block are cut out so that the design stands out in relief. In 1495, Dürer began producing series' of woodcuts; he later also experimented with **etching**, a technique consisting in corroding a metal plate, on which a design has been cut out in an acid-resistant ground, with nitric acid (called at the time "*acqua forte*"); the effect when printed is soft, similar to drawing.

Index

Finito di stampare nel mese di giugno 1998
presso Giunti Industrie Grafiche S.p.A. – Stabilimento di Prato